Summary of

David Epstein's

Range:

Why Generalists Triumph in A Specialized World

Overview & Analysis by

Summary Genie

ISBN
9798639452970

Note to readers:

This is an unofficial summary & analysis of David Epstein's *Range: Why Generalists Triumph in A Specialized World* designed to enrich your reading experience. Please buy the original book through Amazon.

of the Author's knowledge; however, the Author cannot guarantee its accuracy and validity and cannot be held liable for any errors or omissions. Upon using the information contained in this book, you agree to hold harmless the author from and against any damages, costs, and expenses, including any legal fees, potentially resulting from the application of any of the information provided by this guide. The disclaimer applies to any damages or injury caused by the use and application, whether directly or indirectly, of any advice or information presented, whether for breach of contract, tort, neglect, personal injury, criminal intent, or under any other cause of action. You agree to accept all risks of using the information presented inside this book.

The fact that an individual or organization is referred to in this document as a citation or source of information does not imply that the author or publisher endorses the information that the individual or organization provided. This is an unofficial summary & analytical review and has not been approved by the original author of the book.

Your Free Gift!

As a way to say, "**Thank You!**" for being a fan of our summaries, we've included a **Free Gift** for you-a powerful brain program that helps **Increase Your IQ, Memory and Focus _Fast!_**

To receive your free gift, please visit:
http://www.summarygenie.com/freegift

Thank you once again!

The Summary Genie Team

Table of Contents

Summary of Range by David Epstein

Range is the bestselling book by journalist David Epstein, that seeks to address a prevalent myth in our culture about the benefits of early specialization. Starting from the case of two elite athletes, Tiger Woods and Roger Federer, Epstein explores the specialized versus the generalist model.

While both men were unparalleled in their success, there is a major difference between golf and tennis, which serves as the basis for Epstein's subsequent exploration: while golf is a "kind" environment where feedback is immediate and accurate and patterns abound, tennis is a "wicked" environment that requires flexibility and adaptation.

Epstein then expands his research into the realms of music, art, pedagogy, technology, scientific research and innovation, to show how people can benefit from being generalists, being outsiders and getting a supposed "late start" on their career.

Today's culture loves emphatic people who cling to their single narrative; it also prizes long-term thinking as being synonymous with being wise. However, what the research shows – across countless disciplines – is that short-term thinking actually allows people to be happier and satisfied, and that being able to let go of your well trusted tools and pick up new ones is what produces innovation and potentially adverts disaster.

Range is divided into twelve chapters, with an introduction and a conclusion:

Chapter by Chapter Analysis

Introduction: Roger vs. Tiger

Epstein starts his book from the world of sports, with a famous story he thinks his readers already know. At six months old, the baby was already special. He had an amazing sense of balance, and was already walking through the house holding a toy golf club at seven months. At ten months, he was imitating a golf swing. In order to teach his pre-verbal child, his father drew pictures indicating where he should put his hands on the club. At two years old, he was shooting golf balls on Bob Hope's television show.

He entered and won his first competition, competing in the ten and under division. At four years old, the boy was spending eight hours alone at the golf course, and winning serious money off people who bet against him. His father knew he had a golf genius on his hands, and he dedicated all his efforts to his responsibility in bettering him.

Then the author tells another story, this time of someone famous in sports that might not be immediately recognizable. This boy had a soccer coach for a mother, but she never coached him. He liked to kick a ball around with her casually, but he also enjoyed skiing, wrestling, swimming and skateboarding. He also tried basketball, handball, tennis, table tennis, badminton and soccer at school.

His parents had no real athletic goals for him. They just knew that he needed to get his energy out, so they liked to encourage him to try different things. When he started playing tennis, his mother decided not to coach him at it, as he was a frustrating student. His father only had one rule for him when he played: don't cheat. When his coaches wanted to push him ahead, he told them he preferred to play with his friends who were less advanced, as the point of playing was to have fun.

These two men are Tiger Woods and Roger Federer, two of the most accomplished athletes of all time. When the two met at 2006, when they were both at the peak of their powers, they reflected on their differences: while Tiger had "pushy" parents, Roger called his parents "pully," as if they were trying to "pull" him away from the sport; while Tiger had every early advantage, Roger hung back, tried different things, and had fun.

Tiger represents the idea that the quantity of "deliberate practice" determines success and, thus, that it must start as early as possible, like the musical genius Mozart or the programming genius Mark Zuckerberg.

Epstein actually points to a different series of studies that compare elite and near-elite athletes. These studies show on the contrary that while *near*-elite athletes do undergo an intense period of deliberate practice, elite athletes actually go through a youthful "sampling period" where they play a variety of sports in a less structured environment.

This allows them to gain a number of physical proficiencies that acts as a base for their future efforts, and to learn about their talents, so that they can later choose to specialize. This is corroborated by psychological studies that show that true learning is best done slowly, so that information can truly be absorbed. This might mean that in early tests, the person performs poorly and appears to be falling behind, when in fact they are mastering the material more slowly.

This book takes the ideas behind late specialization in order to explain to people how they can maintain the benefits of being a generalist, even as the world increasingly incentivizes and demands hyperspecialization. Tigers are important, but we actually need more Rogers.

Chapter 1 begins with the story of a Hungarian man determined to raise the greatest chess players of all time, by creating a regimented upbringing for his children. They all did very well at chess, but never achieved world dominance.

Epstein questions what it is about things like chess that allow people to specialize in it so profoundly. Talking with psychological experts on the subject, he was able to figure out that the key to building specialization in this way, is choosing an activity like chess that is considered a "kind" learning environment, one in which patterns repeat over and over.

In these environments, players get quick and accurate feedback, and can constantly improve. A game like golf is similar, as the ball moves according to laws of physics within defined boundaries.

The contrast is a "wicked" domain, where the rules are either unclear or incomplete, with feedback that is either delayed, inaccurate or both; there may be patterns, but they may be hidden. This means that a fire fighter who has developed expertise in the situation of house fires would face significant challenges when trying to work in an office building. Tennis shares a similar unpredictability, as there are so many more variables in such a dynamic game, hence the "Roger" phenomenon.

Epstein concludes that while it might be comforting to pretend that life is like a game of chess, it is more like tennis. This means that it is to our benefit to drive down an eight-lane highway and know we have the capacity to switch, rather than sticking to a single lane.

Epstein starts this chapter by discussing the Flynn effect, discovered by a man who had been comparing the results of IQ scores of war veterans from the first and second World Wars. After doing extensive research, he established that every generation has a higher IQ score than the previous one, for an average of three points in ten years.

He explains this striking improvement by the fact that our minds are influenced by the world around us, which makes it easier for people today to solve complex puzzles instantaneously, compared to our ancestors who had "kinder" learning environments and thus, expected to find things today just as they had found them yesterday.

Today, we are exposed to so much more technology, and the related terminology necessary to discuss it, that we absorb this general knowledge without realizing it. We naturally classify our world, and as the world gets more complex, so too to our ways of making sense of it. We are able to do this without prior experience because we have a broader toolkit.

Because of his findings, Flynn was a big proponent of generalized education, especially at the university level. This kind of training is the equivalent of having a mental Swiss Army knife, prepared for any possibility. But he believes schools are falling short, as specialist mentalities tend to prevail.

This chapter leaps back in time to seventeenth-century Venice, a city where music burst from every doorway. In Venice, of all the famed musicians, were a group of women who were basically the equivalent of rock stars: they could improvise all sorts of songs on all sorts of instruments, and people flocked to hear them, including Rousseau.

When he visited them, he was shocked to find out that these girls were disfigured and impoverished: effectively, they were daughters of prostitutes who had been taken off the streets and raised in orphanages, where they were taught music as a way to help increase attendance at church.

Epstein asks, how did they achieve this mastery from such humble origins? Surprisingly, they had relatively few structured, formal lessons, and instead were allowed to experiment on a range of instruments. They were incentivized to learn more instruments, as they were paid separate amounts for each one they learned.

Today, "tiger moms" (and dads) agonize in online forums about what instrument they should pick for their children. They worry about how to force two year olds to enjoy music, and fret that if they have not achieved a certain level by seven, it will be too late. However, even Yo Yo Ma, the great cellist, had a circuitous route to the cello, starting with violin and moving to piano before finding his great love – his "sampling" period just like Roger's.

The real secret to success, musical or otherwise, is to allow your children to experiment and be creative, to find their own voice. In fact, creative children grow up in households with fewer rules, in which parents teach them right and wrong *after* they have allowed them to make some kind of "mistake." This way, the kids are constantly learning.

This chapter starts with a study that was done in math classes across the globe, in order to compare various classroom and learning styles. One of the big things they noticed was that teachers across the globe used two different kinds of questions.

First, "using procedures" questions, means to practice something that was just learned. Second, "making connections" questions, means to connect students to a broader concept, basically asking them to figure out *why* a formula works by testing it out in different ways. Both kinds are useful, but the study showed that it was important to note what teachers did after they asked the connections problem.

Basically, they noticed that teachers liked to help eliminate student confusion. Thus, they would give hints to the point that they would solve the issue, thwarting the true learning that was taking place. In the U.S., teachers asked twenty percent "making connections" problems, but in every single case, they helped so much that the questions turned into a "using procedures" question.

The result of this kind of pedagogy is that U.S. students have a high degree of dependence on memorized algorithms, making them unable to solve basic theoretical math questions.

Another concept that researchers have gleaned is the importance of spacing out lessons, which goes against common pedagogical practices. It states that the most durable learning takes place by allowing time to pass between lessons.

This means that people who learn something quickly, will be able to perform well on a test immediately afterwards, while people who learn slowly, will perform worse. However, when the test is repeated at a distance, the results reverse. Short-term rehearsal of knowledge only gives short-term benefits.

A key way to ensure flexible knowledge is by using a procedure called interleaving, or varied / mixed practice. Interleaving helps improve inductive reasoning. An example might be studying flash cards with images by different painters, but mixing different painters into the stack.

While it will be harder during your practice sessions, when you get to the museum you should be better at identifying the works of the different artists. In a math class, this means learning different kinds of problems instead of group problems together by type. There are similar results in tests involving physical skill as well.

Are you enjoying the book so far?

If so, please help us reach more readers by taking 30 seconds
to write
just a few words on Amazon

Thank you very much!
Now, let's continue…

When Johannes Kepler was inventing astrophysics, he was blazing a completely new trail. In order to try to understand how the planets moved, he had to use analogies, because there was nothing like it in the world he knew.

This kind of thinking, called "deep analogical thinking," means recognizing conceptual similarities across various domains or scenarios, even if they don't seem to have much in common. Analogies are an important tool for solving problems in "wicked" domains, because it forces people to think relationally.

So how can we all be a little more like Kepler in our abilities to use deep analogies? A scientist named Dedre Gentner made up a task called the "ambiguous sorting task." It had twenty-five cards, each that described some actual real world task, like how an economic bubble or an internet router works. Each card has two categories, one for its domain (like economy or technology) and one for its deep structure. Then people are asked to sort the cards.

The people who were best able to sort the cards in a sophisticated way all shared one quality: they had studied an interdisciplinary range of classes. This kind of program is generally not appreciated by professors and departments, who want their students to take focused, specialized classes.

However, such an interdisciplinary curriculum is what leads to the best problem solvers. The price of such interdisciplinary is that people might feel like they are giving up a head start on a career; however, the truly long sighted individuals will realize it is worth it in the end.

This chapter starts with one of the most important artists of the history of the world, Vincent Van Gogh, a man who changed the way artists painted. Van Gough only achieved greatness in the later years of his life, in his late thirties. The same goes for another painter, Paul Gauguin, another one of the few artists whose paintings have sold for more than $100 million.

J.K. Rowling is another famous example of someone who failed in her twenties, and who felt liberated by failure to try to find work that better suited her talents. These successful artists did not succeed in spite of their late start, but because of it.

This idea about trying and failing is integral to understanding how range makes people potentially more successful: testing out career paths is crucial to finding the right one. The secret is to be able to try and fail efficiently, so it becomes possible to move on to something better for that person.

Epstein looks at another problem with quitting, involving West Point Cadets, who clearly have the required grit to get through arduous training. The reason, they discovered, that people were leaving, was that having grit was not a useful selection mechanism to sort out who would be successful in the military, long term. It was just enough to get them through the super intense trials of school.

Now, West Point is trying to allow students more flexibility to allow them to adjust to their own development, rather than pushing them through a standard program like cogs in a machine. The problem is, people are so concerned with the time they have already invested, known as the "sunk cost" that they are unwilling to change paths when they realize they have not chosen the right one.

Epstein starts by telling the story of a woman named Frances Hesselbein who grew up in a small town, and ended up having a remarkable career in business without even graduating college. She simply did what seemed most interested or most needed to her at the time. He then talks to scientists who researched the phenomenon of people who were successful and wandered circuitously around their professional life.

What they all shared in common with Hesselbein was their focus on short term, rather than long term, planning. Paradoxically, the long term plan is actually the more risky one, because it involves being locked into a commitment without knowing what might be best for your future self.

In our culture, we are obsessed with trying to predict how we will grow up, for example, there is the famous marshmallow test that tries to correlate a child's ability to delay gratification with his future success.

However, the reality does not meet the predictions: people change a great deal, in ways they cannot predict. Thus, the "plan and implement" model that people tend to think is best, is really a way to force ourselves into unhappiness.

This chapter looks at people who come into a field without the specific relevant expertise and solve problems that alluded experts, for example the man who figured out a simple method for transporting the sludge that had been cleaned up from the Exxon Valdez mess based on an experience he had pouring concrete for a friend's steps.

The most incredible story, that was the basis for an episode of *This American Life*, is about a woman named Jill who had a rare genetic mutation and was able to do so much investigation, with no formal training, that she was able to change the path of genetic research on that topic. Jill had basically no muscle and no fat on her frame, and she recognized her unusual physique in the body of a Canadian sprinter.

Although no one would believe her at first, she persevered and convinced Epstein to investigate further. Jill had already done a lot of research herself, and thanks to her digging, she diagnosed herself with Emery-Dreifuss disease: she recognized her dad's scrawny arm in a picture in a medical book.

To get herself tested she had to convince an Italian research group to enroll her in a study, but it took years to get a reply that ultimately confirmed her diagnosis. She discovered that she had a rare genetic mutation.

Then, later in life she saw the picture of the Canadian sprinter and wanted to investigate. The sprinter had no fat on her arms, like Jill, but was different from her because she had muscle—lots of it. Eventually she was able to get in contact with Priscilla and find a doctor who would investigate her genes—the same one that Jill had a mutation in.

Jill's hunch proved correct, as both women had the exact same rare subcategory of the genetic mutation. Because of Jill, Priscilla was able to learn valuable medical information about herself, and avoid possible medical complications. Because Jill and Priscilla seemed so different, there is no way that they would have been given the same medical diagnosis.

However, Jill's outsider perspective allowed her to see things in a different way, making valuable use of her intimate, but not "professional," knowledge of her condition. Armed with this information, Jill found the work of a hyperspecialist who works on the protein that helps cells decide whether to use fat from a meal or store it away – in animals, it causes either extreme muscle atrophy or growth.

When Jill contacted him and explained her relationship to Priscilla, it opened the scientist's eyes and changed the path of his research. This story, then, shows the value of the dialogue between specialists who uncover vast amounts of information and dilettantes who figure out new things to do with that information.

Are you enjoying the book so far?

If so, please help us reach more readers by taking 30 seconds
to write
just a few words on Amazon

Thank you very much!
Now, let's continue...

This chapter tells the story about how the Gameboy was invented in Japan, when a businessman saw another man on a train fooling around on his calculator just to relieve his boredom. It gave him the idea that people might like to play on portable devices when they were traveling.

This intersected with a meeting with Sharp, the calculator manufacturer, who was struggling to figure out what to do with their LCD screens now that calculators were no longer a lucrative business.

They decided to use this dirt-cheap technology to try to realize the businessman's vision. In order to figure out how to make the screen a proper resolution, the man used his knowledge of the credit card industry that enabled detailed embossments on plastic surfaces.

Although his device was crude, it had a lot of advantages, in that it was sturdy and durable, with a long lasting battery. The fact that the hardware was old and familiar meant that developers already knew how to make games for it, so the company was able to release hit after hit.

This story of Gameboy is an example of what Epstein calls "lateral thinking with withered technology." Basically, they were able to find novel uses for technology after others had left it behind, giving them a unique edge.

Thanks to the businessman's knowledge of many different sectors, he could think laterally and combine things like the LCD screen and the credit card technology; then there were the experts who were able to do their part on making each component work. The physicist Freeman

Dyson explained the theory as such: we need frogs and birds, focused people and visionary people.

This chapter is about the people who become so entrenched in their big idea about the way the world works that they cling to it, even when they are presented with evidence to the contrary. Our society is very dependent on these people: we put them on the news and on television, and we believe their bad predictions. This is because when experts paint their world view through one narrow keyhole, they make a compelling soundbite, and it becomes easier to quote them.

These experts are known as "hedgehogs" because they go deep and narrow. Foxes, instead, draw on an "eclectic array of traditions" and are able to handle ambiguity and contradiction. Foxes, not surprisingly, are better equipped to make long term predictions because of their willingness to learn and change, but hedgehogs make for better television.

Failure to drop one's familiar tools does not just limit innovation but can also be responsible for deadly accidents, such as the Challenger explosion from the 1980s. The question of why the Challenger was incorrectly allowed to launch ended up coming down, not to a question of having the right information but in clinging to old tools in a situation full of pressure.

They tried to make the unique information fit with the old patters that they knew, and as a result made the fatal error to launch. Although they went "by the book" it turns out the book was wrong. They pushed ahead anyway, rather than throw out the information that clearly did not fit.

This pattern of behavior is called "overlearned behavior," when people do the same thing in response to challenges that it becomes their default that they do not question. Basically, NASA used the wrong tools for the job but were too attached to it to let it go.

This chapter discusses the mindset of the deliberate amateur, focusing on elite scientists who like to do casual experiments in order to push their limits and try new things, often ending up with amazing innovations as a result.

The word amateur used to be a positive word, coming from Latin and meaning someone who loves to do something. Now, however, it is used to belittle people who are not experts.

Today, however, the research shows that deliberate amateurs are often the most successful in their work. A team of researchers looked at the networks that result in creative triumph, and regardless of the sector, they discovered that in order to thrive, teams needed to have porous boundaries between themselves.

When people were isolated, on the contrary, that's where most failure lied. Unfortunately, it is easier to secure funding or get published when you specialize, even though the work that builds bridges between disparate pieces of knowledge is actually the most valuable.

Are you enjoying the book so far?

If so, please help us reach more readers by taking 30 seconds to write
just a few words on Amazon

Thank you very much!
Now, let's continue...

Conclusion: Expanding Your Range

Epstein got two reactions when doing his research on data that suggests that elite athletes do not specialize early. Some people disbelieved him. Others demanded advice: what should we do in light of this knowledge? Epstein wrote this book to answer that question.

He discovered that it is very difficult to tell the story of a successful person and really make it reflect all the twists and turns it takes. It is easier, in retrospect, to tell of someone like Tiger Woods, destined for greatness from birth.

However, the disorderly path of experimentation is the one where creativity and innovation flourish. There is no perfect system people can follow, no simple method that will guarantee success. There are simply highs and lows. In the end, he gives one piece of advice: don't feel behind. Since we don't know exactly where we are headed, there is no point in feeling behind. Just be willing to adjust and learn as you go.

Background Information about *Range*

Range, the bestselling book by David Epstein, has earned rave reviews from a variety of media outlets. *New York Times Book Review* praises it, saying, "The storytelling is so dramatic, the wielding of data so deft and the lessons so strikingly framed that it's never less than a pleasure to read. . ... a wealth of thought-provoking material." NPR called it "a convincing, engaging survey of research and anecdotes that confirm a thoughtful, collaborative world is also a better and more innovative one."

The *Wall Street Journal* lauded it as "A well-supported and smoothly written case on behalf of breadth and late starts. . ... as David Epstein shows us, cultivating range prepares us for the wickedly unanticipated." Even the illustrious Malcolm Gladwell chimed in with words of praise, saying, "For reasons I cannot explain, David Epstein manages to make me thoroughly enjoy the experience of being told that everything I thought about something was wrong.

I *loved Range*." Daniel H. Pink, author of *When, Drive,* and *A Whole New Mind* has this to say about the contribution of *Range,* "For too long, we've believed in a single path to excellence. Start early, specialize soon, narrow your focus, aim for efficiency. But in this groundbreaking book, David Epstein shows that in most domains, the way to excel is something altogether different.

Sample widely, gain a breadth of experiences, take detours, and experiment relentlessly. Epstein is a deft writer, equally nimble at telling a great story and unpacking complicated science. And *Range* is an urgent and important book, an essential read for bosses, parents, coaches, and anyone who cares about improving performance." James Clear, *New York Times* best-selling author of *Atomic Habits*, describes it as "A goldmine of surprising insights. Makes you smarter with every page."

Background information about David Epstein

David Epstein, is a graduate of Columbia University where he earned degrees in environmental science and journalism. He currently is an author and an investigative reporter for *ProPublica* who also worked as a senior writer for *Sports Illustrated.* He is the author of the *New York Times* bestseller *The Sports Gene*, and he has given a TED talk that has had seven million views. He lives in Washington, DC.

Trivia Questions on *Range*

1. Who are the two men that Epstein uses to start his story?

2. Is life more like a tennis game or a golf game, for Epstein?

3. What does the Flynn effect measure?

4. Who invented astrophysics?

5. Where was Gameboy invented?

6. What inspired the creation of Gameboy?

7. Why do we need "frogs" and "birds" in our culture?

8. What are the two kinds of experts and which kind does Epstein prefer?

9. What was the original meaning of amateur?

10. What is Epstein's one sentence of advice?

Discussion Questions on *Range*

1. How does your parenting style compare to Roger and Tiger's parents? Or, if you are not a parent, how did your parents compare to them?

2. How did your education compare to what Epstein describes in the book?

3. What is the most surprising thing you learned in this book?

4. What is one point of disagreement you have with the author about this book?

5. If you could change one thing about your current lifestyle as a result of reading this book, what would it be?

6. Have you ever tried to use analogies to problem solve? How did it help?

7. Do you think you have "range" in your life? Why or why not? How does it help you? How does it create disadvantages?

8. What changes do you think we should make in our school system as a result of Epstein's book?

9. If you could give a friend one piece of advice from this book, what would it be?

10. If you could ask the author one question, what would it be?

Thank You!

We hope you've enjoyed your reading experience. Our team at Summary Genie is constantly striving to deliver to you the highest quality summary guides. We'd like to thank you for supporting us and reading until the very end.

Before you go, would you kindly please leave us a review on Amazon? It would mean a lot to us and it will support our work in creating more high quality summary guides for you in the future.

Thank you once again!

Warmly yours,

The Summary Genie Team

CPSIA information can be obtained
at www.ICGtesting.com
Printed in the USA
BVHW031459281220
596585BV00002B/435